ROUND THE WORLD
IN SPANISH
With Easy Pronunciation Guide

Carol Watson and Dolores Bereijo
Illustrated by David Mostyn

Pronunciation guide by Geoffrey K. Pullum

En la ciudad

la iglesia

el garaje

la casa

el parque

la parada
de autobús

los
semáforos

el paso
de peatones

el anuncio

la señal
de tráfico

el hotel

la fábrica

la tienda

la chimenea

el camarero

el parque
de bomberos

el coche
de bomberos

4

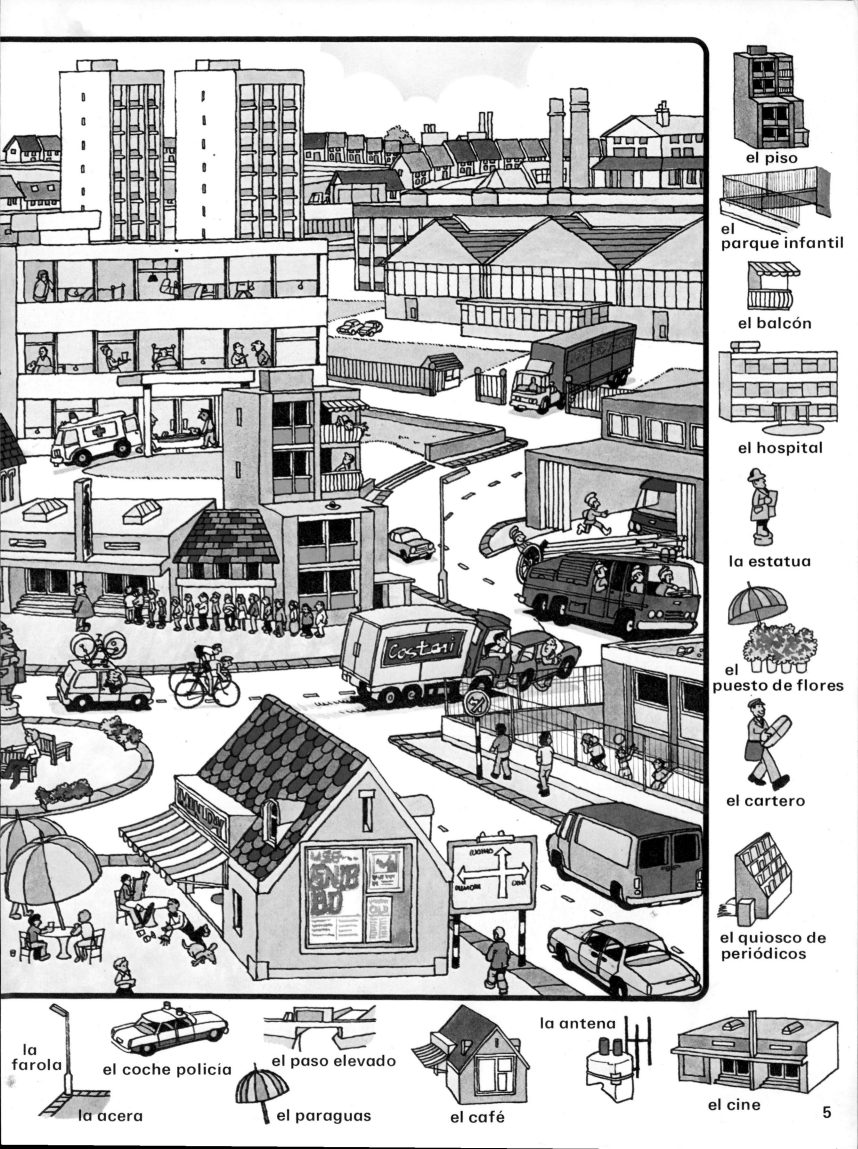

el piso

el parque infantil

el balcón

el hospital

la estatua

el puesto de flores

el cartero

el quiosco de periódicos

la farola

el coche policía

la acera

el paso elevado

el paraguas

el café

la antena

el cine

5

En movimiento

el tren

la rikisha

el biplano

la furgoneta

la bicicleta

el camión para caballerías

el carro de caballos

el globo de aire caliente

el coche deportivo

el autobús

el transportador

el camión cisterna

el hang-glider

el tanque

el monoraíl

el remolque

6

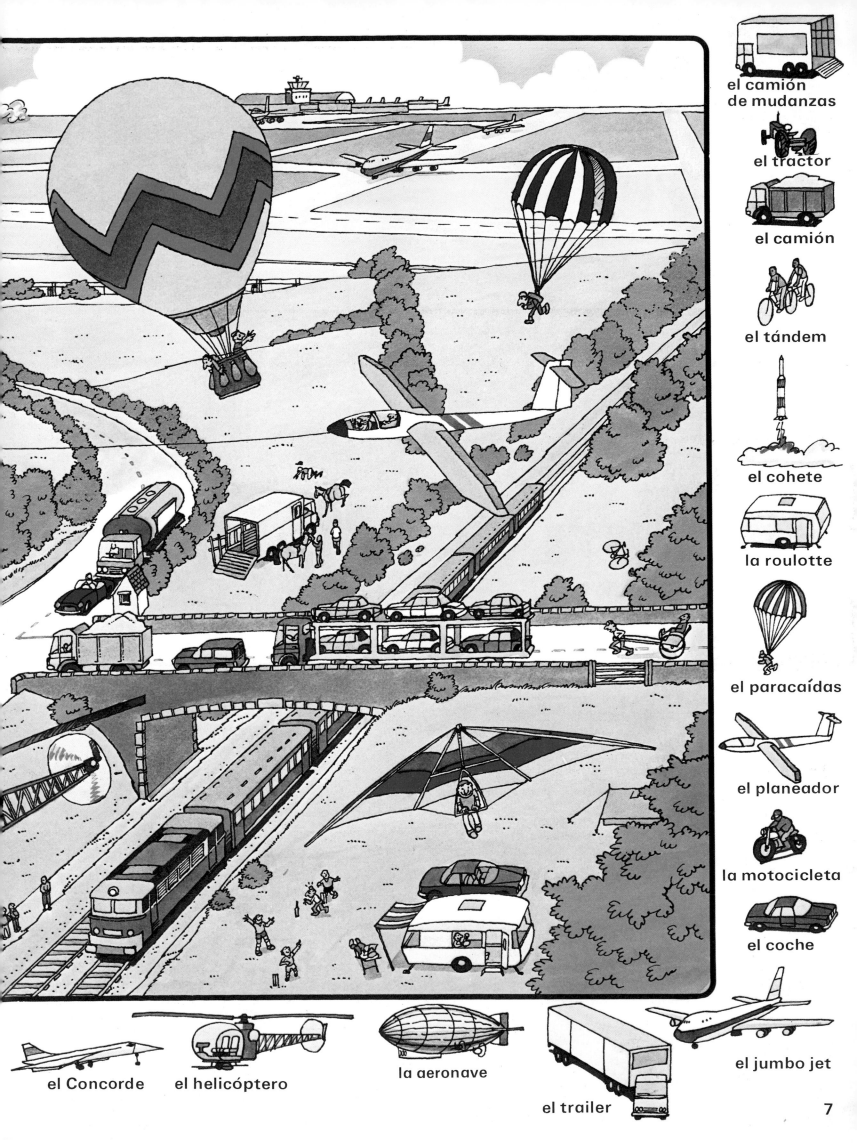

el camión de mudanzas

el tractor

el camión

el tándem

el cohete

la roulotte

el paracaídas

el planeador

la motocicleta

el coche

el jumbo jet

el Concorde

el helicóptero

la aeronave

el trailer

7

la red

el cesto

el río

la presa
pesquera

el canal

las espadañas

la canoa

el puente

la caña

el sedal

el pescador

la tumbona

8

En el agua

la barcaza

el pato

el patito

el acueducto

la balsa

la puerta
de esclusa

la motora

el motor
fuera-bordo

la lancha
neumática

el malecón

el cobertizo
para botes

los juncos

la vivienda
flotante

el canalete

el corcho

el yate de motor

el cisne

el bote de remos

el remo

9

En el puerto

el remolcador

el aerodeslizador

la grúa

el bolardo

el almacén

la boya

el saco

la caja

la portilla

el submarino

el estibador

la gabarra

la chimenea

el transbordador

el envase

la bandera

10

el pesquero

el pescador

el gancho

el ancla

el hidroala

el tanque de depósito

la red

el marinero

los escalones

la vela

el petrolero

el transatlántico

el cajón de embalaje

el bote salvavidas

la draga

el cinturón salvavidas

el bote

11

En la sierra

la roca

el alpinista

la cuerda

la oveja

la cabra

el águila

el pico

el piolet

12 el glaciar

el puma

las piedras

el esquí

el abeto

la cueva

el mapa

el caminante

el telesquí

el canto rodado

la mochila

la cascada

el oso   el osezno

los cuernos

el alce de América

la cabaña de troncos

el bosque

el leñador

los prismáticos

el tronco

las botas de escalar

la sierra

el hacha

13

el burro

la silla
de montar

la rata canguro

el nómada

el camello

el zorro del
desierto

el pozo
petrolífero

el avestruz

el antílope

el halcón

En el desierto

la duna

la arena

el espino

el pozo

la tortuga
del desierto

14

la gacela

el jeep

la palmera

la manta

la calavera

el esqueleto

la culebra

la liebre

el buitre

la hormiga

la tienda

el oasis

el lagarto

el escorpión

el lirio
del desierto

15

el tiburón

la aleta

el pez

la escafandra

las botellas
de oxígeno

la playa

los guijarros

la esponja

la roca

Bajo el agua

el naufragio

el cofre del tesoro

la cuerda

la cueva

la
estrella de mar

16

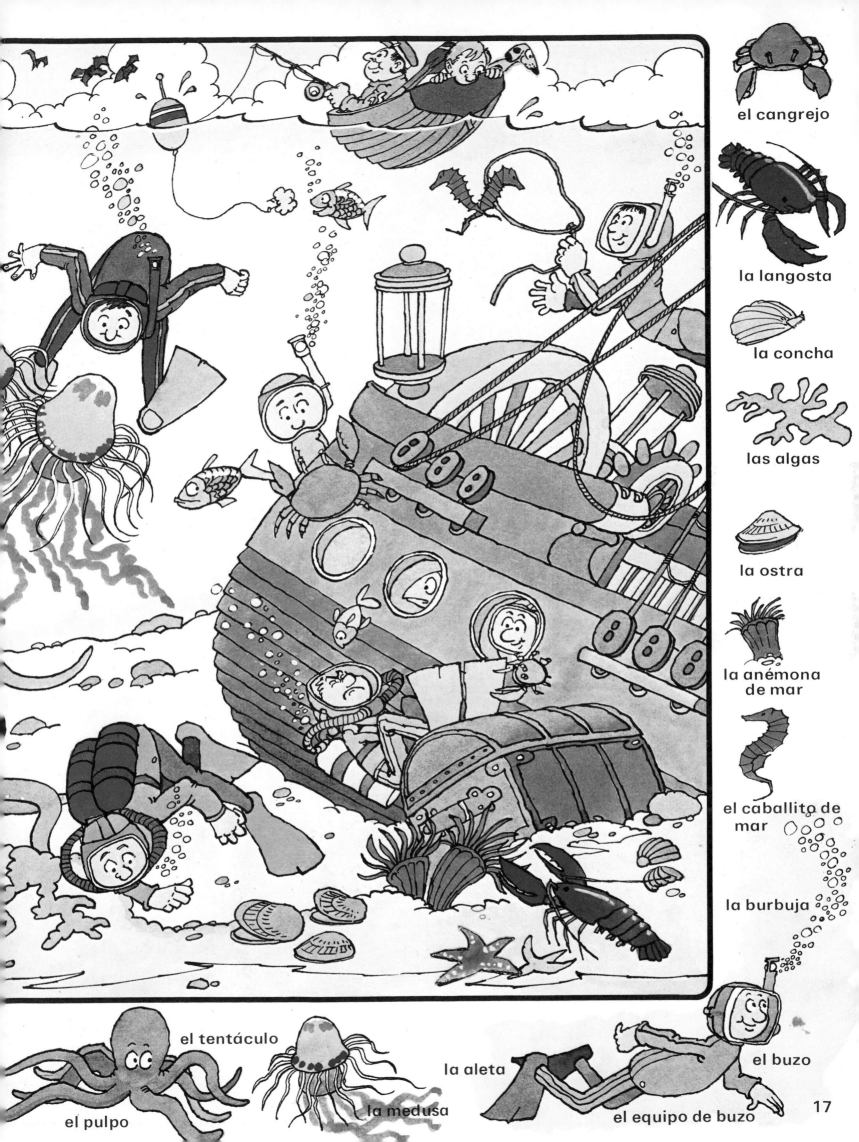

el cangrejo

la langosta

la concha

las algas

la ostra

la anémona
de mar

el caballito de
mar

la burbuja

el buzo

el tentáculo

la aleta

el pulpo

la medusa

el equipo de buzo

17

En la jungla

el gorila

el bambú

la enredadera

el tucán

la araña

la flecha

el cazador

la rana de San Antonio

la mariposa

18   la canoa

el científico

la seta

el jaguar

el chimpancé

el camaleón

la culebra

el murciélago

el tapir

el mono

el cocodrilo

el lémur

el perezoso

el loro

las huellas

la orquídea

el colibrí

el tronco de árbol

la hoja

el puente de cuerdas

el oso hormiguero

19

Tierras frías

el iceberg

el hielo

el perro esquimal

la capucha

el arpón

los anteojos

el carámbano

el muñeco de nieve

la bola de nieve

el iglú

el esquiavión

el rompehielos

la golondrina de mar

la foca

el kayac

20

el reno

la morsa

el oso polar

la nieve

el tractor de nieve

el trineo

la ballena

el zorro blanco

la lechuza blanca

el snow-cat

las raquetas de nieve

las manoplas

el trineo a motor

el esquimal

21

El carnaval

el escudo

el tambor

la hoguera

el aro

el acróbata

la bruja

el malabarista

la peluca

la bufanda

la borla

el estandarte

el penacho

el casco

la máscara

la capa

la linterna

22

los fuegos artificiales

la bailarina

los zancos

el palo de escoba

el payaso

el pendiente

el dosel

la pluma

los globos

la llama

las espuelas

la vela

la lanza

la bandera

el carruaje

23

La música

la trompa

el tambor

los palillos

las castañuelas

la pandereta

el oboe

el triángulo

la guitarra eléctrica

el atril

el director

el órgano

la cítara

el acordeón

la concertina

el xilófono

el bajón

la trompeta

la armónica

el violoncelo

24

la tuba

la balalaica

el violín

el arco

el saxofón

los platillos

el arpa

el dulce

las maracas

la gaita

la campanilla

la guitarra

el trombón

el clarinete

el banjo

la flauta

el contrabajo

el piano

25

Comidas y bebidas

el pincho moruno

la tortita

el perrito caliente

el pavo

el melocotón

las ostras

las patatas fritas

la manzana

el helado

las salchichas de Frankfurt

los espaguetis

la ciruela

la hamburguesa

el pan

la leche

el tomate

el café

26

las fresas

la cerveza

el bocadillo

el queso

el pescado

la empanada

el té

el vino

el pastel

la gelatina

la pera

las cerezas

la limonada

los caracoles

el maíz

el arroz

la ensalada

27

Vestidos

la falda hawaiana

las botas

el kimono

los pantalones vaqueros

la pajarita

el caftán

la gorra

la sotana

la boina

28

la capa

el sombrero hongo

el bolero

las zapatillas

el chal

el sombrero Stetson

la gorrita

el chandal

el sombrero
de copa

el poncho

la
falda escocesa

el sombrero

el sari

el fez

el velo de
musulmana

el hábito

el frac

el turbante

las chaparreras

las sandalias

el esmoquin

el sombrero
de culí

los
zuecos

el
traje espacial

29

Los cultivos

el tabaco

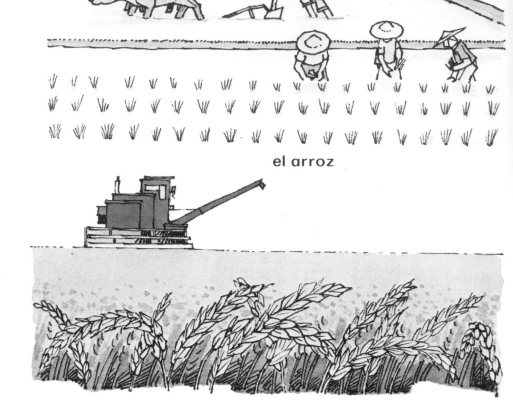

el arroz

los dátiles

el trigo

las coles

los cocos

los tulipanes

el algodón

las uvas

el cacao

el té

las piñas

los girasoles

el café

la madera

la caña de azucar

los plátanos

31

Peligros

el iceberg

las arenas movedizas

el maremoto

el volcán

el terremoto

el huracán

la tromba marina

el incendio forestal

la avalancha

el relámpago

la ventisca

el tornado

la tempestad de arena

la inundación

33

Casas y viviendas

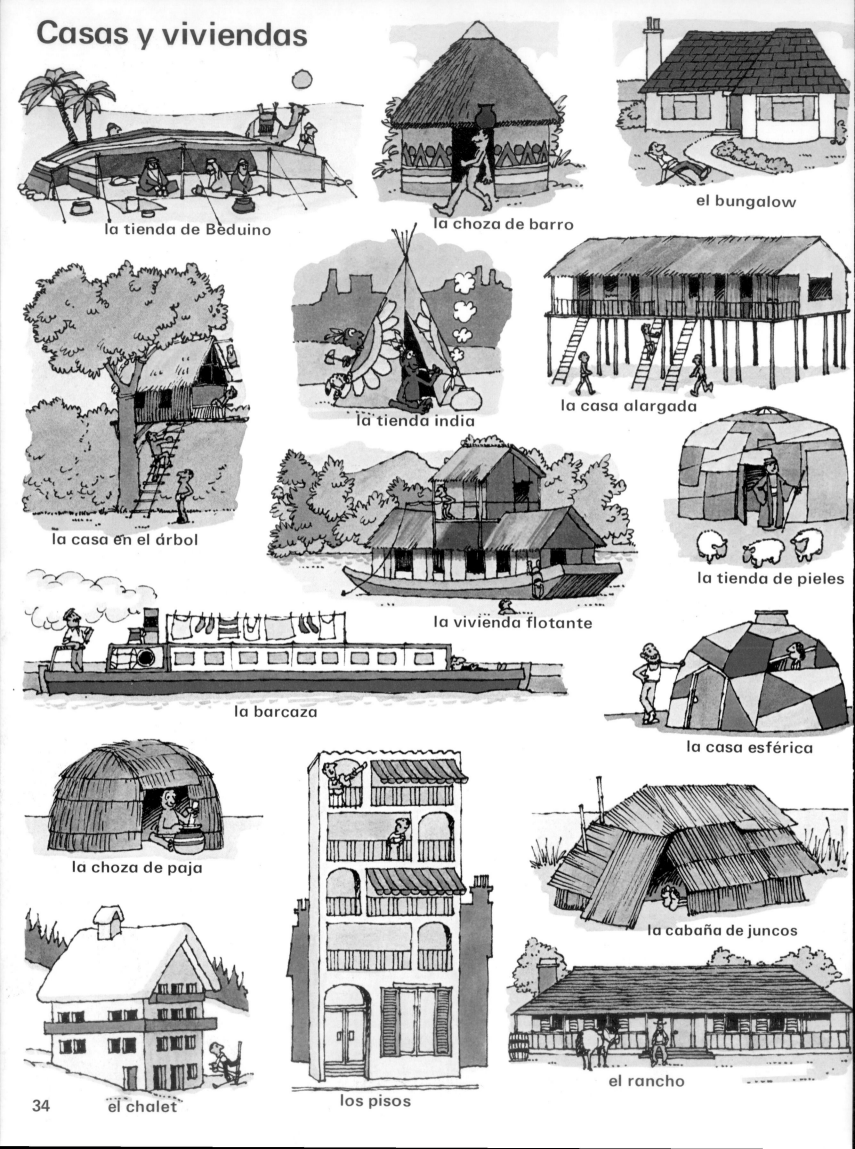

la tienda de Beduino

la choza de barro

el bungalow

la casa en el árbol

la tienda india

la casa alargada

la vivienda flotante

la tienda de pieles

la barcaza

la casa esférica

la choza de paja

la cabaña de juncos

el chalet

los pisos

el rancho

la casa de papel

el faro

la granja

la cueva

el carro de gitanos

la casita de campo

el palafito

el castillo

el fuerte

la cabaña de troncos

el sampán

la casa urbana inglesa

35

Animales

el orangután

el bisonte

el wombat

el coala

el tití

el león

el castor

el yak

el galápago

el hipopótamo

el mapache

la cebra

el delfín

el elefante

el tejón

la ardilla listada

el gibón

36

el panda gigante

la llama

el tigre

la mofeta

el ñu

el lémur

el puerco-espín

el armadillo

la hiena

el mandril

el canguro

la jirafa

el lobo

el leopardo

el rinoceronte

37

Edificios y lugares famosos

1 el castillo de Luis de Baviera
— Alemania

2 el puente 'Puerta de Oro'
— América

3 la torre inclinada de Pisa
— Italia

4 la Mezquita Azul
— Irán

5 el palacio de la ópera de Sydney
— Australia

6 las cataratas del Niágara
— América y Canadá

7 el Everest
— Nepal

8 la Torre Eiffel
— Francia

9 Stonehenge (monumento neolítico)
— Inglaterra

10 la catedral de San Basilio
— Rusia

11 el templo de Taj Mahal
    – la India

12 una Pirámide y la Esfinge
    – Egipto

13 el Gran Cañón del Colorado
    – América

14 la Torre de Londres
    – Inglaterra

15 el Partenón
    – Grecia

16 la Estatua de la Libertad
    – América

17 el Coliseo
    – Roma

18 Cabo Kennedy
    – América

19 el Templo del Paraíso
    – China

Look at the map on the next two pages. Match up the numbers to find out where the buildings and places are in the world.

El mapamundi

ALASKA — el esquimal

GROENLANDIA — el iglú

OCÉANO ÁRTICO — el barco de pesca

CANADÁ

6

ESTADOS UNIDOS DE AMÉRICA — el cohete

el aerodeslizador

2   13

16

18

9 14   8   1   EUROPA   3   17   15

el Concorde

OCÉANO ATLÁNTICO

AFRICA

12

SUDAMÉRICA

el transatlántico

OCÉANO PACÍFICO

el bote

Can you name the animals?

40   You can find them in this book.

The numbers on the map show where the famous buildings and places are to be found. See pages 38 and 39.

el globo de aire caliente

RUSIA

OCÉANO PACÍFICO

el maremoto

el submarino

19

CHINA

7

4

11

el pozo petrolífero

LA INDIA

el petrolero

el jumbo jet

AUSTRALIA

NUEVA ZELANDA

el helicóptero

el rompehielos

LA ANTÁRTIDA

el snowcat

Index

This is the alphabetical list of all the words in the pictures in this book. The Spanish alphabet is a little different to English. All words beginning with **ch** come at the end of the **c**'s. Words beginning with **ll** are at the end of the **l**'s and words beginning with **ñ** at the end of the **n**'s. The Spanish word comes first, then there is the pronunciation in *italics,* followed by the English translation.

The pronunciation guide shows how the words are pronounced in Spain. (In Latin America it is a little bit different.) The sounds of Spanish are not exactly the same as the sounds of English, so the only way to pronounce Spanish in exactly the right way is to listen to Spanish people speaking and imitate them. However, the following list will be some help in getting the sounds roughly correct.

ah — stands for a sound like the *a* in *calm*
eh — stands for a sound like the *e* in *get*
oh — stands for a sound like the *o* in *so*

ee — stands for a sound like the *ee* in *seen*
oo — stands for a sound like the *oo* in *soon*
au — roughly rhymes with the *ow* of *cow*
ai — roughly rhymes with the *i* of *fine*
th — always sounds like the *th* of *thin* (never like *the*)
s — always sounds like the *s* of *so* (never like *rose*)
y — always sounds like the *y* of *yes* (never like *my*)
g — always sounds like the *g* of *go* (never like *George*)
kh — stands for a sound like the *ch* of *loch* the way Scots people pronounce it.

There are two different r-sounds:
r — stands for a short r-sound made with one flap of the tongue.
rr — is like the r-sound you use to say *brr!* when it is very cold

It is important to stress the right part of the word in Spanish, so the stressed part of each word is shown in capital letters.

el abeto	*el ah-BEH-to*	fir tree
la acera	*lah ah-THEH-rah*	pavement
el acordeón	*el ah-kor-deh-OHN*	accordion
el acróbata	*el ah-KROH-bah-tah*	acrobat
el acueducto	*el ah-kweh-DOOK-toh*	aqueduct
el aerodeslizador	*el ah-eh-roh-des-leeth-ah-DOHR*	hovercraft
la aeronave	*lah ah-eh-roh-NAH-beh*	airship
Africa	*ah-FREE-kah*	Africa
el agua	*el AH-gwah*	water
el águila	*el AH-gwee-lah*	eagle
Alaska	*ah-LAH-skah*	Alaska
el alce de America	*el AHL-theh deh ah-MEH-ree-kah*	moose
Alemania	*ah-leh-MAHN-yah*	Germany
la aleta	*lah ah-LEH-tah*	fin, flipper
las algas (f)	*lahs AHL-gahs*	seaweed
el algodon	*el ahl-goh-DON*	cotton
el almacén	*el ahl-mah-THEHN*	warehouse
el alpinista	*el ahl-pee-NEES-tah*	climber
el ancla	*el AHNG-klah*	anchor
la anémona de mar	*lah ah-NEH-moh-nah deh MAHR*	sea anemone
los animales (m)	*lohs ah-nee-MAH-lehs*	animals
La Antártida	*lah ahn-TAHR-tee-dah*	Antarctica
la antena	*lah ahn-TEHN-ah*	aerial
los anteojos (m)	*lohs ahn-teh-OH-khohs*	goggles
el antílope	*el ahn-TEE-loh-peh*	antelope
el anuncio	*el ah-NOON-thee-oh*	advertisement
la araña	*lah ah-RAHN-yah*	spider
el árbol	*el AHR-bohl*	tree
el arco	*el AHR-koh*	bow
la ardilla listada	*lah ahr-DEE-lyah lees-TAH-dah*	chipmunk
la arena	*lah ah-REH-nah*	sand
las arenas movedizas (f)	*lahs ah-REH-nahs moh-beh-DEE-thahs*	quicksand

el armadillo	*el ahr-mah-DEE-lyoh*	armadillo
la armónica	*lah ahr-MOH-nee-kah*	harmonica
el aro	*el AH-ro*	hoop
el arpa	*el AHR-pah*	harp
el arpón	*el ahr-POHN*	harpoon
el arroz	*el ah-RROHTH*	rice
el atril	*el ah-TREEL*	music stand
Australia	*au-STRAH-lyah*	Australia
el autobús	*el au-toh-BOOS*	bus
la avalancha	*lah ah-bah-LAHN-cha*	avalanche
el avestruz	*el ah-beh-STROOTH*	ostrich
la bailarina	*lah bai-lah-REE-nah*	dancer
bajo	*BAH-kho*	under
el bajón	*el bah-KHON*	bassoon
la balalaica	*lah bah-lah-LAI-kah*	balalaika
el balcón	*el bahl-KOHN*	balcony
la balsa	*lah BAHL-sah*	raft
la ballena	*lah bah-LYEH-nah*	whale
el bambú	*el bahm-BOO*	bamboo
la bandera	*lah bahn-DEH-rah*	flag
el banjo	*el BAHNG-khoh*	banjo
la barcaza	*lah bahr-KAH-thah*	canal barge
el barco de pesca	*el BAHR-koh deh PES-kah*	fishing boat
la bebida	*lah beh-BEE-dah*	drink
la bicicleta	*lah bee-thee-KLEH-tah*	bicycle
el biplano	*el bee-PLAH-noh*	bi-plane
el bisonte	*el bee-SOHN-teh*	bison
el bocadillo	*el boh-kah-DEE-lyoh*	sandwich
la boina	*lah BOH-ee-nah*	beret
la bola de nieve	*lah BOH-lah deh nee-EH-beh*	snowball
el bolardo	*el boh-LAHR-doh*	bollard
el bolero	*el boh-LEH-roh*	bolero
la borla	*lah BOHR-lah*	tassel

el bosque	*el BOHS-keh*	forest
la bota	*lah BOH-tah*	boot
las botas (f)	*lahs BOH-tahs*	boots
las botas de escalar (f)	*lahs BOH-tahs deh ehs-kah-LAHR*	climbing boots
el bote	*el BOH-teh*	dinghy
el bote de remos	*el BOH-teh deh REH-mohs*	rowing boat
el bote salvavidas	*el BOH-teh sahl-vah-VEE-dahs*	lifeboat
las botellas de oxígeno (f)	*lahs boh-TEH-lyahs deh ohk-SEE-kheh-noh*	aqualung
la boya	*lah BOH-yah*	buoy
la bruja	*lah BROO-khah*	witch
la bufanda	*lah boo-FAHN-dah*	scarf
el buitre	*el BWEE-treh*	vulture
el bungalow	*el boong-GAH-loh*	bungalow
la burbuja	*lah boor-BOO-khah*	bubble
el burro	*el BOO-rroh*	donkey
el buzo	*el BOO-thoh*	diver
el caballito de mar	*el kah-bah-LYEE-toh deh MAHR*	seahorse
la cabaña de juncos	*lah kah-BAH-nyah deh KHOONG-kohs*	reed house
la cabaña de troncos	*lah kah-BAH-nyah deh TROHNG-kohs*	log cabin
Cabo Kennedy	*KAH-boh KEH-neh-dee*	Cape Kennedy
la cabra	*lah KAH-brah*	goat
el cacao	*el kah-KAH-oh*	cocoa
el café	*el kah-FEH*	café, coffee
el caftán	*el kahf-TAHN*	kaftan
la caja	*lah KAH-khah*	box
el cajón de embalaje	*el kah-KHOHN deh em-bah-LAH-kheh*	crate
la calavera	*lah kah-lah-BEH-rah*	skull
el camaleón	*el kah-mah-leh-OHN*	chameleon
el camarero	*el kah-mah-REH-roh*	waiter
el camello	*el kah-MEH-lyoh*	camel
el caminante	*el kah-mee-NAHN-teh*	walker
el camión	*el kah-mee-OHN*	lorry
el camión cisterna	*el kah-mee-OHN thee-STEHR-nah*	petrol tanker
el camión de mudanzas	*el kah-mee-OHN deh moo-DAHN-thahs*	removal van
el camión para caballerías	*el kah-mee-OHN pah-rah kah-bah-lyeh-REE-ahs*	horsebox
la campanilla	*lah kahm-pah-NEE-lyah*	hand bell
Canadá	*kah-na-DAH*	Canada
el canal	*el kah-NAHL*	canal
el canalete	*el kah-nah-LEH-teh*	paddle
el cangrejo	*el kahng-GREH-khoh*	crab
el canguro	*el kahng-GOO-roh*	kangaroo
la canoa	*lah kah-NOH-ah*	canoe
el canto rodado	*el KAHN-toh roh-DAH-doh*	boulder
la caña	*lah KAH-nyah*	rod
la caña de azucar	*lah KAH-nyah deh ah-thoo-KAHR*	sugar cane
la capa	*lah KAH-pah*	cloak
la capucha	*lah kah-POO-chah*	hood
el caracol	*el kah-rah-KOHL*	snail
los caracoles (m)	*lohs kah-rah-KOH-lehs*	snails
el carámbano	*el kah-RAHM-bah-noh*	icicle
el carnaval	*el kahr-nah-VAHL*	carnival
el carro de caballos	*el KAH-rroh deh kah-BAH-lyohs*	horse and cart
el carro de gitanos	*el KAH-rroh deh khi-TAH-nohs*	gypsy caravan
el carruaje	*el kah-roo-AH-kheh*	carriage
el cartero	*el kahr-TEH-roh*	postman
la casa	*lah KAH-sah*	house
la casa alargada	*lah KAH-sah ah-lahr-GAH-dah*	long house
la casa de papel	*lah KAH-sah deh pah-PEL*	paper house
la casa en el árbol	*lah KAH-sah en el AHR-bohl*	tree house
la casa esférica	*lah KAH-sah ehs-FEH-ree-kah*	dome house
la casa urbana inglesa	*lah KAH-sah oor-BAH-nah ing-GLEH-sah*	terraced house
casas y viviendas	*KAH-sahs ee bee-BYEHN-dahs*	houses and homes
la cascada	*lah kahs-KAH-dah*	waterfall
el casco	*el KAHS-koh*	helmet
la casita de campo	*lah kah-SEE-tah deh KAHM-poh*	cottage
las castañuelas (f)	*lahs kah-stah-NYWEH-lahs*	castanets
el castillo	*el kah-STEE-lyoh*	castle
el castillo de Luis de Baviera	*el kah-STEE-lyoh deh loo-EES deh bah-BYEH-rah*	Ludwig's Castle
el castor	*el kah-STOHR*	beaver
las cataratas del Niágara (f)	*lahs kah-tah-RAH-tahs del nee-AH-gah-rah*	Niagara Falls
la catedral de San Basilio	*lah kah-teh-DRAHL deh sahn bah-SEE-lyoh*	St Basil's Cathedral
el cazador	*el kah-thah-DOHR*	hunter
la cebra	*lah THEH-brah*	zebra
la cereza	*lah theh-REH-thah*	cherry
las cerezas (f)	*lahs theh-REH-thahs*	cherries
la cerveza	*lah thehr-BEH-thah*	beer
el cesto	*el THEHS-toh*	hamper
el científico	*el thyen-TEE-fee-koh*	scientist
el cine	*el THEE-neh*	cinema
el cinturón salvavidas	*el theen-too-ROHN sahl-bah-BEE-dahs*	lifebelt
la ciruela	*lah theer-WEH-lah*	plum
el cisne	*el THEES-neh*	swan
la cítara	*lah THEE-tah-rah*	sitar
la ciudad	*lah thee-oo-DAHD*	city
el clarinete	*el klah-ree-NEH-teh*	clarinet
el coala	*el koh-AH-lah*	koala bear
el cobertizo para botes	*el koh-behr-TEE-thoh pah-rah BOH-tehs*	boathouse
el coco	*el KOH-koh*	coconut
el cocodrilo	*el koh-koh-DREE-loh*	crocodile
el coche	*el KOH-cheh*	car
el coche de bomberos	*el KOH-cheh deh bohm-BEH-rohs*	fire engine
el coche deportivo	*el KOH-cheh deh-pohr-TEE-boh*	sports car
el coche policía	*el KOH-cheh poh-lee-THEE-ah*	police car
el cofre del tesoro	*el KOH-freh del teh-SOH-roh*	treasure chest

el cohete	*el koh-EH-teh*	rocket
la col	*lah KOHL*	cabbage
las coles (f)	*lahs KOH-lehs*	cabbages
el colibrí	*el koh-lee-BREE*	humming bird
el Coliseo	*el koh-lee-SEH-oh*	The Colosseum
la comida	*lah koh-MEE-dah*	food
comidas y bebidas	*koh-MEE-dahs EE beh-BEE-dahs*	food and drink
la concertina	*lah kohn-thehr-TEE-nah*	concertina
el Concorde	*el kohn-KOHR-deh*	Concorde
la concha	*lah KOHN-chah*	shell
el contrabajo	*el kohn-trah-BAH-khoh*	double bass
el corcho	*el KOHR-choh*	float
la cuerda	*lah KWEHR-dah*	rope
los cuernos (m)	*lohs KWEHR-nohs*	antlers
la cueva	*lah KWEH-bah*	cave house, cave
la culebra	*lah koo-LEH-brah*	snake
los cultivos (m)	*lohs kool-TEE-bohs*	crops
el chal	*el CHAHL*	shawl
el chalet	*el chah-LEHT*	chalet
el chandal	*el CHAHN-dahl*	tracksuit
las chaparreras (f)	*lahs chah-pah-RREH-rahs*	chaps
la chimenea	*lah chee-meh-NEH-ah*	chimney, funnel
el chimpancé	*el cheem-pahn-THEH*	chimpanzee
China	*CHEE-nah*	China
la choza de barro	*lah CHOH-thah deh BAH-rroh*	mud hut
la choza de paja	*lah CHOH-thah deh PAH-kha*	grass hut
los dátiles (m)	*lohs DAH-tee-lehs*	dates
el delfín	*el del-FEEN*	dolphin
el desierto	*el deh-SYEHR-toh*	desert
el director	*el dee-rek-TOHR*	conductor
el dosel	*el doh-SEHL*	canopy
la draga	*lah DRAH-gah*	dredger
el dulce	*el DOOL-theh*	recorder
la duna	*lah DOO-nah*	dune
el edificio	*el eh-dee-FEE-thee-oh*	building
edificios y lugares famosos	*eh-dee-FEE-thee-ohs ee loo-GAH-rehs fah-MOH-sohs*	famous buildings and places
Egipto	*eh-KHEEP-toh*	Egypt
el elefante	*el eh-leh-FAHN-teh*	elephant
la empanada	*lah em-pah-NAH-dah*	pie
la enredadera	*lah en-reh-dah-DEH-rah*	creeper
la ensalada	*lah en-sah-LAH-dah*	salad
el envase	*el en-BAH-seh*	container
el equipo de buzo	*el eh-KEE-poh deh BOO-thoh*	wetsuit
la escafandra	*lah ehs-kah-FAHN-drah*	mask (of a diver)
los escalones (m)	*lohs ehs-kah-LOH-nehs*	steps
el escorpión	*el eh-skohr-PYOHN*	scorpion
el escudo	*el eh-SKOO-doh*	shield
el esmoquin	*el eh-SMOH-keen*	tuxedo
las espandañas (f)	*lahs eh-spah-DAH-nyahs*	bulrushes
los espaguetis (m)	*lohs eh-spah-GEH-tees*	spaghetti
el espino	*el eh-SPEE-noh*	thornbush
la esponja	*lah eh-SPOHNG-khah*	sponge
las espuelas (f)	*lahs eh-SPWEH-lahs*	spurs
el esqueleto	*el eh-skeh-LEH-toh*	skeleton
el esquí	*el eh-SKEE*	ski
el esquiavión	*el eh-skee-ah-BYOHN*	ski plane
el esquimal	*el eh-skee-MAHL*	Eskimo
Estados Unidos de América (E.E.U.U.)	*eh-STAH-dohs oo-NEE-dohs deh ah-MEH-ree-kah (eh eh oo oo)*	United States of America
el estandarte	*el eh-stahn-DAHR-teh*	banner
la estatua	*lah eh-STAH-twah*	statue
la Estatua de la Libertad	*lah eh-STAH-twah deh lah lee-behr-TAHD*	The Statue of Liberty
el estibador	*el eh-stee-bah-DOHR*	docker
la estrella de mar	*lah eh-STREH-lyah deh MAHR*	starfish
Europa	*eh-oo-ROH-pah*	Europe
el Everest	*el eh-beh-REHST*	Mount Everest
la fábrica	*lah FAH-bree-kah*	factory
la falda escocesa	*lah FAHL-dah eh-skoh-THEH-sah*	kilt
la falda hawaiana	*lah FAHL-dah ah-wah-YAH-nah*	grass skirt
famoso	*fah-MOH-soh*	famous
el faro	*el FAH-roh*	lighthouse
la farola	*lah fah-ROH-lah*	lamp post
el fez	*el FEHTH*	fez
la flauta	*lah FLAU-tah*	flute
la flecha	*lah FLEH-chah*	arrow
la foca	*lah FOH-kah*	seal
el frac	*el FRAHK*	tailcoat
Francia	*FRAHN-thyah*	France
la fresa	*lah FREH-sah*	strawberry
las fresas (f)	*lahs FREH-sahs*	strawberries
frío	*FREE-oh*	cold
los fuegos artificiales (m)	*lohs FWEH-gohs ahr-tee-fee-thee-AHL-ehs*	fireworks
el fuerte	*el FWEHR-teh*	fort
la furgoneta	*lah foor-goh-NEH-tah*	van
la gabarra	*lah gah-BAH-rrah*	barge
la gacela	*lah gah-THEH-lah*	gazelle
la gaita	*lah GAI-tah*	bagpipes
el galápago	*el gah-LAH-pah-goh*	giant tortoise
el gancho	*el GAHN-choh*	hook
el garaje	*el gah-RAH-kheh*	garage
la gelatina	*lah kheh-lah-TEE-nah*	jelly
el gibón	*el khee-BOHN*	gibbon
los girasoles (m)	*lohs khee-rah-SOH-lehs*	sunflowers
el glaciar	*el glah-THYAHR*	glacier
el globo	*el GLOH-boh*	balloon
el globo (de aire caliente)	*el GLOH-boh (deh AI-reh kahl-YEN-teh)*	hot air balloon
la golondrina de mar	*lah goh-lohn-DREE-nah deh MAHR*	tern
el gorila	*el goh-REE-lah*	gorilla
la gorra	*lah GOH-rrah*	cap
la gorrita	*lah goh-RREE-tah*	bonnet
el Gran Cañón del Colorado	*el GRAHN kah-NYOHN del koh-loh-RAH-doh*	The Grand Canyon
la granja	*lah GRAHNG-khah*	farmhouse
Grecia	*GREH-thyah*	Greece

Spanish	Pronunciation	English
Groenlandia	groh-ehn-LAHN-dyah	Greenland
la grúa	lah GROO-ah	crane
el guijarro	el gee-KHAH-rroh	pebble
los guijarros (m)	lohs gee-KHAH-rrohs	pebbles
la guitarra	lah gee-TAH-rrah	guitar
la guitarra electrica	lah gee-TAH-rrah eh-LEHK-tree-kah	electric guitar
el hábito	el ah-BEE-toh	habit
el hacha	el AH-chah	axe
el halcón	el ahl-KOHN	hawk
la hamburguesa	lah ahm-boor-GEH-sah	hamburger
el hang glider	el ahng-glee-DEHR	hang glider
el helado	el eh-LAH-doh	ice cream
el helicóptero	el eh-lee-KOHP-teh-roh	helicopter
el hidroala	el ee-droh-AH-lah	hydrofoil
el hielo	el YEH-loh	ice
la hiena	lah YEH-nah	hyena
el hipopótamo	el ee-poh-POH-tah-moh	hippopotamus
la hoguera	lah oh-GEH-rah	bonfire
la hoja	lah OH-khah	leaf
la hormiga	lah ohr-MEE-gah	ant
el hospital	el oh-spee-TAHL	hospital
el hotel	el oh-TEL	hotel
las huellas (f)	lahs WEH-lyahs	tracks
el huracán	el oo-rah-KAHN	hurricane
el iceberg	el ee-theh-BEHRG	iceberg
la iglesia	lah ee-GLEH-syah	church
el iglú	el ee-GLOO	igloo
el incendio forestal	el een-THEHN-dyoh foh-reh-STAHL	forest fire
India	EEN-dyah	India
Inglaterra	eeng-glah-TEH-rrah	England
la inundación	lah een-oon-dah-THYOHN	flood
Irán	ee-RAHN	Iran
Italia	ee-TAH-lyah	Italy
el jaguar	el kha-GWAHR	jaguar
el jeep	el KHEEP	jeep
la jirafa	lah khee-RAH-fah	giraffe
el jumbo jet	el KHOOM-boh KHEHT	jumbo jet
los juncos (m)	lohs KHOONG-kohs	reeds
la jungla	lah KHOONG-glah	jungle
el kayac	el kah-YAHK	kayak
el kimono	el kee-MOH-noh	kimono
el lagarto	el lah-GAHR-toh	lizard
la lancha neumática	lah LAHN-chah neh-oo-MAH-tee-kah	rubber dinghy
la langosta	lah lahng-GOH-stah	lobster
la lanza	lah LAHN-thah	spear
la leche	lah LEH-cheh	milk
la lechuza blanca	lah leh-CHOO-thah BLAHNG-kah	snowy owl
el lémur	el LEH-moor	lemur
el leñador	el leh-nya-DOHR	lumberjack
el león	el leh-OHN	lion
el leopardo	el leh-oh-PAHR-doh	leopard
la liebre	lah lee-EH-breh	hare
la limonada	lah lee-moh-NAH-dah	lemonade
la linterna	lah leen-TEHR-nah	lantern
el lirio del desierto	el LEE-ryoh del deh-SYEHR-toh	desert lily
el lobo	el LOH-boh	wolf
el loro	el LOH-roh	parrot
el lugar	el loo-GHAHR	place
la llama	lah LYAH-mah	flame, llama
la madera	lah mah-DEH-rah	timber
el maíz	el mah-EETH	corn
el malabarista	el mah-lah-bah-REE-stah	juggler
el malecón	el mah-leh-KOHN	jetty
el mandril	el mahn-DREEL	baboon
las manoplas (f)	lahs man-NOH-plahs	mittens
la manta	lah MAHN-tah	blanket
la manzana	lah mahn-THAH-nah	apple
el mapa	el MAH-pah	map
el mapache	el mah-PAH-cheh	racoon
el mapamundi	el mah-pah-MOON-dee	map of the world
las maracas (f)	lahs mah-RAH-kahs	maracas
el maremoto	el mah-reh-MOH-toh	tidal wave
el marinero	el mah-ree-NEH-roh	sailor
la mariposa	lah mah-ree-POH-sah	butterfly
la máscara	lah MAH-skah-rah	mask
la medusa	lah meh-DUH-sah	jellyfish
el melocotón	el meh-loh-koh-TOHN	peach
La Mezquita Azul	lah mehth-KEE-tah ah-THOOL	The Blue Mosque
la mochila	lah moh-CHEE-lah	haversack
la mofeta	lah moh-FEH-tah	skunk
el mono	el MOH-noh	monkey
el monorail	el moh-noh-RAIL	monorail
la morsa	lah MOHR-sah	walrus
la motocicleta	lah moh-toh-thee-KLEH-tah	motorcycle
el motor fuera-bordo	el moh-TOHR FWEH-rah BOHR-doh	outboard motor
la motora	lah moh-TOH-rah	motorboat
el movimiento	el moh-bee-MYEHN-toh	movement
el muñeco de nieve	el moo-NYEH-koh deh nee-EH-beh	snowman
el murciélago	el moor-thee-EH-lah-goh	bat
la música	lah MOO-see-kah	music
el naufragio	el nau-FRAH-kyoh	wreck
Nepal	neh-PAHL	Nepal
la nieve	lah nee-EH-beh	snow
el nómada	el NOH-mah-dah	nomad
Nueva Zelanda	NWEH-bah theh-LAHN-dah	New Zealand
el ñu	el NYOO	gnu
el oasis	el oh-AH-sees	oasis
oboe	el oh-BOH-eh	oboe
Océano Artico	oh-THEH-ah-noh ahr-TEE-koh	Arctic Ocean
Océano Atlántico	oh-THEH-ah-noh aht-LAHN-tee-koh	Atlantic Ocean
Océano Pacifico	oh-THEH-ah-noh pah-THEE-fee-koh	Pacific Ocean
el orangután	el oh-rahng-oo-TAHN	orang-utan
el órgano	el OHR-gah-noh	organ
la orquídea	lah ohr-KEE-deh-ah	orchid
el osezno	el oh-SEHTH-noh	bear cub
el oso	el OH-soh	bear

Spanish	Pronunciation	English
el oso hormiguero	el OH-soh ohr-mee-GEH-roh	anteater
el oso polar	el OH-soh poh-LAHR	polar bear
la ostra	lah OH-strah	oyster
las ostras (f)	lahs OH-strahs	oysters
la oveja	lah oh-BEH-kha	sheep
la pajarita	lah pah-khah-REE-tah	bow tie
El Palacio de la ópera de Sydney	el pah-LAH-thyoh deh lah OH-peh-rah deh SEED-nee	The Sydney Opera House
el palafito	el pah-lah-FEE-toh	stilthouse
los palillos (m)	lohs pah-LEE-lyohs	drumsticks
la palmera	lah pahl-MEH-rah	palm tree
el palo de escoba	el PAH-loh deh eh-SKOH-bah	broomstick
el pan	el PAHN	bread
el panda gigante	el PAHN-dah khee-GAHN-teh	giant panda
la pandereta	lah pahn-deh-REH-tah	tambourine
los pantalones vaqueros (m)	lohs pahn-tah-LOH-nehs bah-KEH-rohs	jeans
el paracaídas	el pah-rah-kah-EE-dahs	parachute
la parada de autobús	lah pah-RAH-dah deh au-toh-BOOS	bus stop
el paraguas	el pah-RAH-gwahs	umbrella
el parque	el PAHR-keh	park
el parque de bomberos	el PAHR-keh deh bohm-BEH-rohs	fire station
el parque infantil	el PAHR-keh een-fahn-TEEL	playground
el Partenón	el pahr-teh-NOHN	The Parthenon
el paso de peatones	el PAH-soh deh peh-ah-TOH-nehs	crossing
el paso elevado	el PAH-soh eh-leh-BAH-doh	flyover
el pastel	el pah-STEHL	gateau
las patatas fritas (f)	lahs pah-TAH-tahs FREE-tahs	chips
el patito	el pah-TEE-toh	duckling
el pato	el PAH-toh	duck
el pavo	el PAH-boh	turkey
el payaso	el pah-YAH-soh	clown
el peligro	el peh-LEE-groh	danger
la peluca	lah peh-LOO-kah	wig
el penacho	el peh-NAH-choh	plume
el pendiente	el pehn-DYEHN-teh	earring
la pera	lah PEH-rah	pear
el perezoso	el peh-reh-THOH-soh	sloth
el perrito caliente	el peh-RREE-toh kah-lee-EHN-teh	hotdog
el perro esquimal	el PEH-rroh eh-skee-MAHL	husky dog
el pescado	el peh-SKAH-doh	fish
el pescador	el peh-skah-DOHR	fisherman
el pesquero	el peh-SKEH-roh	fishing boat
el petrolero	el peh-troh-LEH-roh	oil tanker
el pez	el PEHTH	fish
el piano	el PYAH-noh	piano
el pico	el PEE-koh	peak
la piedra	lah PYEH-drah	stone
las piedras (f)	lahs PYEH-drahs	stones
el pincho moruno	el PEEN-choh moh-ROO-noh	shish kebab
la piña	lah PEE-nyah	pineapple
el piolet	el pyoh-LEHT	ice axe
Pirámide y la Esfinge	pee-RAH-mee-deh ee lah ehs-FEENG-kheh	Pirámide and the Sphinx
el piso	el PEE-soh	flat,
los pisos (m)	lohs PEE-sohs	flats
el planeador	el plah-neh-ah-DOHR	glider
los plátanos (m)	lohs PLAH-tah-nohs	bananas
los platillos (m)	lohs plah-TEE-lyohs	cymbals
la playa	lah PLAH-yah	sand (beach)
la pluma	lah PLOO-mah	feather
el poncho	el POHN-choh	poncho
la portilla	lah pohr-TEE-lyah	porthole
el pozo	el POH-thoh	well
el pozo petrolífero	el POH-thoh peh-troh-LEE-feh-roh	oil well
la presa pesquera	lah PREH-sah peh-SKEH-rah	weir
los prismáticos (m)	lohs prees-MAH-tee-kohs	binoculars
el puente	el PWEHN-teh	bridge
el puente de cuerdas	el PWEHN-teh deh KWEHR-dahs	rope bridge
el puente ''Puerta de Oro''	el PWEHN-teh PWEHR-tah deh OH-roh	The Golden Gate Bridge
el puerco espín	el PWEHR-koh ehs-PEEN	porcupine
la puerta de esclusa	lah PWEHR-tah deh eh-SKLOO-sah	lockgates
el puerto	el PWEHR-toh	harbour, port
el puesto de flores	el PWEH-stoh deh FLOH-rehs	flower stall
el pulpo	el POOL-poh	octopus
el puma	el POO-mah	puma
el queso	el KEH-soh	cheese
el quiosco de periódicos	el kee-OH-skoh deh pehr-YOH-dee-kohs	newspaper stand
la rana de San Antonio	lah RAH-nah deh SAHN ahn-TOHN-yoh	tree frog
el rancho	el RAHN-choh	ranch house
las raquetas de nieve (f)	lahs rah-KEH-tahs deh nee-EH-beh	snowshoes
la rata canguro	lah RAH-tah kahng-GOO-roh	kangaroo rat
la red	lah REHD	net
el relámpago	el reh-LAHM-pah-goh	lightning
el remo	el REH-moh	oar
el remolcador	el reh-mohl-kah-DOHR	tug
el remolque	el reh-MOHL-keh	trailer
el reno	el REH-noh	reindeer
el rikisha	el ree-KEE-sah	rickshaw
el rinoceronte	el ree-noh-theh-ROHN-teh	rhinoceros
el río	el REE-oh	river
la roca	lah ROH-kah	rock
el rompehielos	el rohm-peh-YEH-lohs	icebreaker
la roulotte	lah roh-oo-LOH-teh	caravan
Rusia	ROO-syah	Russia
el saco	el SAH-koh	sack
las salchichas de Frankfurt (f)	lahs sahl-CHEE-chahs deh frahngk-FOORT	frankfurters
el sampán	el sahm-PAHN	sampan
las sandalias (f)	lahs sahn-DAHL-yahs	sandals
el sari	el SAH-ree	sari